DEDICATION

This is Nashville is dedicated to my family-Seth, Owen and LC for always being up for adventures with me! And to Music City for always giving us something fun to explore!

Food trucks and annual festivals take over the streets

> THE LINE WRAPS AROUND PANCAKE PANTRY FOR HOT SYRUPY, PANCAKE STACKS

Pancake Pantry

50 YEARS & Still 23 Varieties

At Iroquois Steeplechase, you'll see horses racing around the track

THERE'S NOWHERE ELSE I'D RATHER BE

About the Author

Lifestyle and family blogger Dawn Burns calls Nashville, Tennessee home, where she is a mother of two and wife to husband, Seth. Dawn has always had a growing love for community and an even stronger passion for families traveling to her beloved city. Striving to connect others with the happenings in Music City and all it has to offer. Dawn, the face behind The Nashville Mom, has become the #1 resource for families in and around Nashville to discover the best restaurants, shops, kid-friendly activities and events in town.

About the Illustrator

Candler Reynolds is a native of Montgomery Alabama, but after a few twists and turns she now calls Nashville, Tennessee home sweet home. Candler's passion for people, process, and creative design infiltrates everything she does, and her free spirit has manifested itself in her art and her curiosity for all things colorful, creative, and life-giving. When she isn't working her full-time job as a graphic designer in Franklin, she is jet setting on the weekends to paint live events and weddings or working on custom commissions for new clients. Regardless of the project, Candler loves to create and believes that her own creativity is a mirror of the creativity of her Creator.

Acknowledgements

Thank you to the businesses and locations included in this book that allowed us to use their names and likeness.

I Believe in Nashville mural used with License permission from I Came Uninvited, LLC.

Jeff McMillen for working your magic!

www.ingramcontent.com/pod-product-compliance
Lightning Source LLC
LaVergne TN
LVHW060811191224
799093LV00001B/1